Let's Have Fun Outside!

LET'S GO TO THE BEACH

By Kristen Rajczak Nelson

Gareth Stevens
PUBLISHING

Please visit our website, www.garethstevens.com. For a free color catalog of all our high-quality books, call toll free 1-800-542-2595 or fax 1-877-542-2596.

Library of Congress Cataloging-in-Publication Data

Names: Rajczak Nelson, Kristen, author.
Title: Let's go to the beach / Kristen Rajczak Nelson.
Description: Buffalo, New York : Gareth Stevens Publishing, [2025] |
    Series: Let's have fun outside! | Includes index.
Identifiers: LCCN 2023045712 | ISBN 9781482465839 (library binding) | ISBN
    9781482465822 (paperback) | ISBN 9781482465846 (ebook)
Subjects: LCSH: Beaches–Juvenile literature. | Summer–Juvenile
    literature. | Outdoor recreation for children–Juvenile literature.
Classification: LCC GB453 .R33 2025 | DDC 551.45/7–dc23/eng/20231012
LC record available at https://lccn.loc.gov/2023045712

Published in 2025 by
Gareth Stevens Publishing
2544 Clinton Street
Buffalo, NY 14224

Copyright © 2025 Gareth Stevens Publishing

Designer: Claire Zimmermann
Editor: Kristen Nelson

Photo credits: Cover, pp. 1, 23 CandyRetriever/Shutterstock.com; p. 5 Nina Buday/
Shutterstock.com; p. 7 fotohunter/Shutterstock.com; pp. 9, 23 (middle) Bilanol/Shutterstock.com;
p. 11 Tatevosian Yana/Shutterstock.com; p. 13 Zack Frank/Shutterstock.com; p. 15 FamVeld/
Shutterstock.com; pp. 17, 24 (left, right) Cliff Day/Shutterstock.com; p. 19 Chris Niemann/
Shutterstock.com; p. 21 Mbuso Sydwell Nkosi/Shutterstock.com.

Printed in the United States of America

Some of the images in this book illustrate individuals who are models. The depictions do not imply actual situations or events.

CPSIA compliance information: Batch #CSGS25: For further information contact Gareth Stevens, at 1-800-542-2595.

Find us on

Contents

It is a hot summer day.
The sun is shining.
Let's go to the beach!

5

Grandma has
a beach bag.
She packs towels.
She packs toys!

I put on my bathing suit.
I wear sandals.

I put on sunscreen.
This keeps my skin safe.

11

The beach is
on the ocean.
It is made of sand.
The sand feels soft!

We put our feet
in the water.
We jump and play
in the waves!

I look for seashells.
I find a white one.
I put it in my bucket.

I see a bird.
It is a seagull!

I make a friend.
His name is James.
We build a sandcastle!

21

The beach is
so much fun!

Words to Know

bucket   sandals   seashell

Index